DROP
FORGED
LENNON

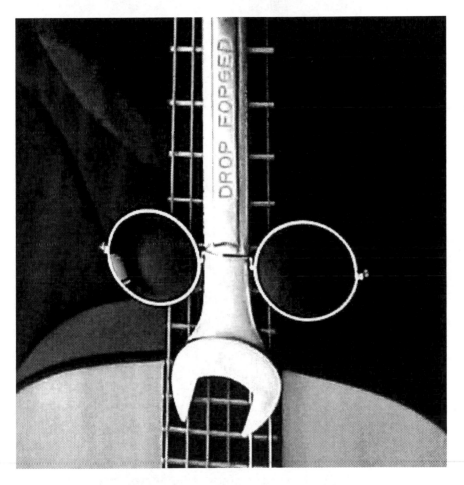

SHARON RICHARDS

Copyright © 2001 by Sharon Richards

ISBN 0-7414-0804-X

Published by:

INFI∞ITY
PUBLISHING.COM

Infinity Publishing.com
519 West Lancaster Avenue
Haverford, PA 19041-1413
Info@buybooksontheweb.com
www.buybooksontheweb.com
Toll-free (877) BUY BOOK
Local Phone (610) 520-2500
Fax (610) 519-0261

Printed in the United States of America

Printed on Recycled Paper

Published September, 2001

TABLE OF CONTENTS

My Deepest Gratitude

This book is dedicated to my poor husband who had to listen to all of my fervent drivel about John. Your patience and tolerance as a mild Beatles fan is much appreciated Stan! You hold this book in your hands because he knew I had the foolish courage to imagine I could be a dreamer. He knew I was not the only one.

CHAPTER

TO

FACT

Memories, Oh Memories!

I was only five months old when they first appeared on the Ed Sullivan show in February of 1964. I'm already jealous of my brother because he was just about to turn four. My heart ached as he described on the phone to me once his "Beatles" memory. "We were at Aunt Muriel's house in Chicago. The girl cousins were screaming- mostly for Paul. I remember them telling me who my favorite Beatle was. Oh it's Paul one would say. Another would say no John, no George. " (goodness even four-year-olds couldn't escape this pressing question!). Well nobody asked me! Actually, no one ever did ask me this question until recently. So that was my brother. I have spoken to people who were "the age" when Beatlemaina reigned supreme. I didn't want to get weird or anything, but I'd like to grill some of these folks for about eight hours each and suck every drop of their Beatles memories and somehow feel that via the inquisition I had experienced it myself. I had the happy fortune to talk with someone I worked with for nearly eight years about her experience at the second Shea Stadium concert. Although I didn't show it completely, I was in awe. To only see the things she saw, the four standing on stage together in their matching suits. Little tiny specs in the sea of adoring fans. I asked only, "Could you hear them?" She said, quite matter of fact, "Yeah, sure." I was amazed. This is the thing that bothers me about reading accounts of their careers. The general feeling among those who never saw them in concert take for fact that they couldn't be heard. Well, I guess you can't believe everything you read. You don't have to believe me either but that's what she told me. Oh, how I wanted to leap to extended discussion and inquiry, but alas, I did not grill her to a pulp. How could you do that to another person? Anyway, they'd get me locked up I'm sure. That is part of the advantage of being a current adult maniac. You can hear these stories and be interested and ask a few questions but you don't start foaming at the mouth. It's just not socially acceptable. Then the kicker she told me was that she used to be a maniac ("Red Alert") and that when she went to college she threw it all- ALL- away. Oh the tragedy of it all! "It just didn't mean anything anymore, I guess I outgrew it." she shrugged. I was in shock and had no response.

OK enough of that! What was my first Beatle memory? I was four. (Not unlike my brother for remembering things.) It was 1968 and "Yellow Submarine" was in theaters. Don't ask me why, I did not see it at the time but I remember Ringo being my favorite Beatle. Obviously, this is not true anymore for me in 2001. Anyway, for quite some time I was mildly into Ringo. My next memory probably dates back to 1978, as I became interested in the Beatles in a post break up sort of way. The late show was an excellent venue for my discovery of the Beatles. I clearly remember seeing "A Hard Day's Night" in the seventies a couple of times on WGN television in Chicago on the late show and even one New Years Eve as a double feature with the Marx Brother's "Duck Soup". Being a mild fan at the time I didn't get the connection of reference, the Beatles to the Marx Brothers, time would bring that eventually. Perhaps I was aware of the Beatles throughout my life in the level of understanding that I could handle. First as cartoons, then as comedians singing music, then post Anthology, but more on that later. I really did not get most of the jokes in "A Hard Day's Night" then and sadly did fall asleep that particular New Year's (I think it was 1978) before they got to the concert. Of course the error of my ways has been corrected multiple times with a punishing series of repeated viewings. A tough job but I had to do it (Oh BooHoo). Let me say that "Naratum Verbatum" is not a disease limited to the youth of our nation. It strikes adults too. For now I can nearly recite all the scenes with my favorite Beatle. Well, I did warn you... I am a maniac.

After that particular New Year, I'm not sure how, I latched on to a nickname. That name was "Max". I have a brass belt buckle to attest to that name and I used to carry a silver hammer around, albeit small, in my pocket. Though I never sought to bang, bang anyone on the head with it. I carried it as a tribute to the Beatles. I liked the song because it was a funny and bouncy tune. My favorite Beatle called it a "Grandma Song". What I supposed turned me off from wanting to be called "Max" and liking the song was when I stopped to realize what it was truly about, only on the surface though, the story it told I mean. A deviate banging people on the head when he doesn't get his way. Then, goes to jail but bangs the judge on the head before the words of Max's sentence leave the judge's lips. Of course the error of that distaste has been assuaged as I have read <u>A Hard Day's</u> <u>Write</u>. Paul only meant to reference that just when things seemed to go OK something comes to ruin it.

I suppose that's why I appreciate them so now. For now I am able to completely comprehend the full scope of their work from the earliest cover songs and influences of their early days to the issues they wrestled with right to the end. Also, the sad comprehension of the immense talent sacrificed when "the devil's best friend" (to quote George) committed his heinous act. I was only seventeen when John was shot and I remember well the silence we observed in class the day of the memorial service. I had purchased several reissue 45 records and had gotten the "Red" album and the Sergeant Pepper picture disc in the late seventies as Christmas gifts. My preference for the Beatles early and middle hits still in its formative stages, the death of John caused me to be more attentive to his come back songs. I purchased nearly all the 45's released after his death and they appear on endless tape recordings I made for myself to play on my new "Walkman". Recalling the size and weight of my first walkman in relation to my current one brings a smile to my face. How technology has changed! That's another subject though.

When the Anthology came out in 1995 I was glued and even watched it in Jacksonville, FL, at my in-laws, on Thanksgiving Day that evening. Fortunately, I was also recording it at home in Orlando. I already had the first two nights on tape. The memories, probably enhanced, came back to me of my early childhood, my teenage time as "Max" and my favorite Beatle, Ringo. Though the recollections had faded the desire to hear the music had been sparked by the Anthology. I picked up the first disc right after it was released, collected the CD's I already had into a pile to review. "Sgt. Pepper" I had purchased back in 1987 (20 years ago today, right?) thus, my husband and I confined ourselves to enjoying these discs. 1995, I would have to say, is when my husband and I appreciated the Beatles at the same level. Then like a dormant bug bite (how trite that is) August of 1996 found hubby and I taking home CD's from his cousins in Tampa. We had been staying with them while we participated in a craft show at the Expo Center in Hillsborough County.

Upon my return to my full-time work on Monday I popped in the disc "A Hard Day's Night"- that's when the early stages of mania set in. I found myself excited by the songs of a distant time. No longer was I inclined to fall asleep as John sang "If I Fell". I was thrilled to have somehow remembered the songs to such a degree as to recall lyrics, tunes and the scenes from the movie in which they appeared. Over the next few months and into 1997 we began to collect the entire CD releases (British) of the original twelve albums. (I with more voracious appetite than my spouse.) We acquired all the Anthology discs, which had come out during 1996 while my bug still lay partially dormant. Part of the reason the dormancy dominated was our financial situation. We simply did not possess the funds to spend on such things. However, when there is a will, and when that will becomes overpowering, a way is found. Soon small bits of profit were siphoned from the craft business account to fund the budding Beatlemania collection. Initially, the purchases filled the holes in our CD collection. Then, since nothing stays the same, things got better. More craft shows, more profit, more money and a new job for my spouse. The economics of the situation were still tight but finding pockets of wealth to funnel to what has become an urge to acquire has become easier. Books were first rented from the Public Library, then purchased on sale only or discount if worthy of owning. Then the most amazing discovery- Beatlefest- the CATALOG! Now the source was exposed and the maniac in me was at a near orgasmic state. I bought more books in 1997, trading cards, selected period memorabilia yet the cost conscious pauper that was still inside kept me from any outlandish splurge.

In 1998, I met my connection with period memorabilia. I know that fate must've had something to do with it. Why do I say fate? Because by pure chance in December of 1997 I heard about a show in Orlando called the FX show. It was advertised on television as a toy and collectibles show. I didn't know it then but it was the largest of its kind in the Southeast. My son in tow, on January 10th I went in the first room I saw. It was carpeted and for the sake of my four-year-old son, thankfully had restrooms. Parents remember and note dumb things like that you know. Anyway... What were the odds! I walked around this literally packed room with dealers and other customers looking at several tables. Of course Star Wars was all over the place and my son, Dan, was quite excited about that. For the first time I got to see the Hallmark Christmas ornaments, from 1996 I think, of the Bealtes. They never do get John quite right though. Ringo always, Paul often, George occasionally and John rarely. Seeing the price I knew then I was not a complete full merchandise maniac either. I'm not sure I am yet but I do know that I am at least a bit more involved than the fan who just listens to their music a lot. Then rounding the corner after seeing what I considered some rip off prices on some memorabilia, (Original stuff looking rather shabby in some cases.) I came across a dealer who said he had a copy of "Life" magazine August of 1964. He would not mail it to me from the northeast which was where he had his shop. I had to get to him! How irritating is that? I did buy a base set of the 1996 issue Beatle trading cards. Don't care for the style of the card much. I prefer the River Group set from 1995. Now having had a few disappointments, I came to the row in the back of the carpeted room and spied a vendor with a few memorabilia items. ZING! Like a magnet! I was sucked into this booth. Looking past the happy meal premiums and toys of the 70's, I saw a vein of gold: Original Period Beatles Memorabilia! It wasn't long before I excitedly introduced myself and voiced my intense liking for the mentioned goods. Then this wonderful, once avid, now mild, Beatles fan said that he had a basement chock full of this stuff and he wanted to get rid of quite a bit of it. Then fate of all fates, as there is only a 25% chance you will meet another fan of the same Beatle you like, his favorite was John! Oh Yeah! Oh Yeah!

So I spent who knows how long at his booth. I literally camped out, seating myself on the carpet in the corner of his booth to see all there was to see and knowing it was only the tip of his memorabilia iceberg. I could only imagine what the rest of the collection was like. What I saw were many good things in my mind. If this was his OK stuff WOW! What else?! Again though, I did not go nuts on a spending spree as it were. I only spent $85.00 and he gave my son a Star Wars puzzle block from a recent Taco Bell promotion. Since I was a fan collecting for the sake of what I liked and not for profit, the dealer told me he was inclined to sell to me at a better price than if I was just buying to turn a profit. Like any fan on the road to fanaticism, I feel I will NEVER sell these things but one never knows. For now though I am buying for the love of it all. Then to find a fellow John fan, who is willing to part with his treasures, for a bargain no less, is the living end for me. Still I am cautioned with him too. As mentioned earlier I do not want to overpower him by being maniacal and talking just about John and sucking the fellow's mind of his Beatle memories for endless hours. I really don't want him to think I'm too weird. Now, you ask, why do I feel fate had something to do with all this? Because after my transaction with him, I wandered about with my son, not seeing anything akin to what he had and then found out that the show actually extended into a much larger room without carpet and what seemed eternal rows of merchandise.

Already pooped out Dan and I did go into the large room but did not see everything and not too much more in Beatle goods that excited me. So how was it that I sort of went in the back door to find the best match for my needs? Not only that but to find a John fan who was kind enough not to want to rip me off. It would've been easy, my weakness so very obvious. FATE! is my reply. In a more bizarre mood I might be inclined to say the spirit of "The Beatles" or John led me to that booth. Though I think that's when most folks would say, "OK now enough is enough! Get away from me you disturbed, silly person". Presently, I have an entire account set up just for the purpose of funding my Beatle habit. Yes, I realize it sounds like I am addicted to some drug but I can think of much worse things to be addicted to.

Dedication

A true dedication
To my life's inspiration
Someone who lived recently

You'd like to know who?
I'm sure you do
Know this person
I'll give you some clues

Some thought him profane
Others declared him insane
But when you first knew him
This wasn't so plain

He had charm and wit
Sharp, sometimes cynical and yet
His sense of humor
A bit crass at times

Do you recall what he said?
His message is not dead
Yes! You remember
In the back of your head

It was all you did need
Such a shame the world won't heed
To this day
What he knew all along

Sure at times he did not
But you forgave him a lot
His only crime was telling the truth
(All he wanted from us)

It was living his heart
That set him apart
Yet one mistook him as false
Forcing at gunpoint his demise

And when taken from here
Late and cold in the year
You know two decades have passed
Since that time

No longer here
We mourned with so many tears
And his name I am certain
You now realize

"It was John Lennon!", you exclaim!
And LOVE was his game
"It's easy", he said
If you try

Can you see what he meant?
Imagine living life in peace it went
Join the dreamers
And see through his eyes

Imagine Love
That's all we need do
Then watch the dream
Come true

And you see he's not gone
He's been here all along
Living life
Through the dreamers
You and me

A True Story

What is the most precious piece in your collection? Not most valuable but most precious. You may say it is the most expensive piece. It's no secret that Beatles memorabilia is a huge market and as pieces change hands from original owners to second, fifth and on down the line a little may get added to that price at each exchange. Certainly the days of the .10 bubble gum cards are gone for good, unless their next trip is to the dustbin. Yet think, which piece is your most precious? What is its story? What follows is mine.

1998: I had been collecting seriously for a couple of years. I already had many magazines, books, period memorabilia and enough photographs, posters and what-not of the Beatles hanging on the walls of my home office to make the great circular room devoted to them at the Hard Rock Café in Orlando look Spartan by comparison. February 1999: in the planning stages for our trip to England, I naturally had thought to search for my ultimate piece while in the "Mother country". I had been on the search for a circa 1963-64 John Lennon signature since early in '97. I had read several articles and informative buyer bewares in price guides. I nearly bought a very appealing autograph of John's at a Beatles Festival one year but couldn't part with a sum just shy of my monthly mortgage payment. Now, within weeks of our departure, I fancied to pick one up in London or Liverpool but on the nearly eight hour flight, I decided I would not consciously look for one, there was surely so much more to enjoy.

A trip of economy by no means, I wanted to get the most fun for my hard earned (and well-spent) money. The much-anticipated vacation to England was about to begin. We landed at Gatwick Airport on a rather typical cloudy day in late May of '99. My husband joked; this was my equivalent of the pilgrim's journey to Mecca. I wasn't about to disagree, their music means so much to those who listen and listen and listen… We lingered in London for a few days seeking out Beatles sites and taking in all the traditional royal landmarks. Then we traveled northward, by train, (scenes of "A Hard Days Night" flashing in my brain) to spend four glorious days in the celebrated birthplace of the Fab Four- Liverpool! Our travel agent had even, unknowingly, booked us at the Adelphi, now Brittania Adelphi Hotel. Arriving mid-morning we set out after lunch toward the Albert Docks, knowing the Beatles Story was there. Having had such a good time so far I'd completely forgotten about the search. We wandered through shops and venues displaying Beatles collectibles. I purchased a few books, some postcards and we did all those things Beatles fans do whilst in Liverpool: Magical Mystery Tour, Cavern Walks, drinking in the very famous Grapes Pub.

We also visited the very famous Beatles Shop on Mathews Street. Descending into the dripping-with-memorabilia walls AND ceiling I was greeted with a cheerful "Ohy!" by the shop's manager. This place even put MY home shrine to shame! Soaking it in I slowly absorbed all I was viewing. My spouse calls it "Sharon's heaven". Indeed! Finally, I engaged the manager in conversation. In our discussion, I recalled I had been on a search for Beatles Monthly magazines. Like any avid collector, I always carried the list of magazines I needed in my collection. I mentioned I had this list with me and he said that he loved a woman with a list. So for the next two hours, my spouse, obediently perching himself on the mock cavern stage in front of my favorite Beatle- John, I filled out my Fab Four fan magazine collection. As the pile grew, I'm not sure specifically how it came up; I mentioned my search for the 63-64 Lennon signature. Now for whatever reason, the manager recalled a local man who might have something in his collection that I would be interested in. Thank goodness for his memory. The manager placed the call and I was to meet this man the next day at The Beatles Shop- 10am. By next morning, I was quite excited but somehow remained contained as we feasted on a traditional English breakfast. Now ready to walk off the hearty food, we headed out on a self-guided walking tour and to the shop, to meet the man who had the piece I might be "interested in". Ten o'clock that morning couldn't arrive soon enough, but we had a delightful time discovering the sites on our self-guided tour.

When we did get to the shop, my Beatles radar in high gear, we met with the gentleman as agreed. He hefted an armload of goods on the counter and I was fascinated to say the least. What he showed me first though was, as the manager of The Beatles Shop confirmed, a valid 62 early 63 signature of John Lennon's. I was terribly attracted to the piece but kept the screaming thirteen year-old at bay in my head. I was mildly surprised and slightly disappointed when he said he came down only to show it to me and that he may not be ready to let go of the piece just yet. "Perhaps at a later date?", I asked, nonchalantly. "Possibly", he said. He showed me the other items, mostly paper: magazines, Mersey Beats and other newspaper clippings. Common fare to the residents of Liverpool, to me, rare pieces I had never seen the likes of back home. I chose a few as we chatted on. I guess he sensed my sincere passion for the band and in particular for John. Somehow, I felt so drawn to the signature. Though John had only signed his first name- a detraction to most collectors he had shown it to- it had other attributes I found highly appealing. In addition, the provenance was quite another story in itself.

This man was the second owner of the autograph, having purchased it from the original owner. He had committed the full provenance to memory, which I immediately recorded to my laptop that night after our second day of Beatles discovery. The reverse of the autograph was an unpublished photo of John with a young blonde girl (obviously a fan) but not the young lady that this man had purchased the piece from. Marie said it was a traded photo. In the heyday of the Beatles time at the Cavern, girls would get themselves photographed with one,

13

two or all of the Beatles. These photos then became something akin to the Pokemon trading cards of today. Though I suspect these had an immense personal value beyond that of a picture of an animated Japanese pocket monster. This young lady (Marie) had traded a picture of herself with one of the other Beatles for the said photo this man had of the blonde girl with John. Marie then took this photo, possibly with four others, up to John at the Cavern and had him sign the backs of each. I've never had the fortunate opportunity to see them live, much less at the Cavern. Then thinking to be able to approach one of them for a signature and five at that, just made the piece all the more intriguing to me. Can you imagine! I was so pleased he was sharing the story.

What was written on the back, true enough, was only John's first name but a few other items along with that made it a remarkable piece in my eyes. Prior to this time, I had only seen John's doodle of his face appear in books with much later signatures, circa 69 and into the early 70's. As we all know John even used only that face doodle to represent his name at times. This was a face doodle with the signature- without glasses and short hair! I was amazed declaring this must be one of the first ever face doodles with his signature. More than that it was exciting because at this point in their careers they still included the kisses after they signed. Three "X's" placed under his name the last marks he made on the back of the photo before the self-portrait doodle. To make the piece even more personal to the recipient, John addressed it "To Marie" and adding in sign off with "many a love from John". The notation "No. 5" would seem to indicate that Marie's was the last of the photos she had him sign. The man said Marie explained she had another photo of John that started "To Gail (No. 2)" though that one did not have his face doodle.

So there I was in Liverpool, my "virgin" visit, staring at an absolutely irresistible autograph from my favorite Beatle and merely knowing it existed I knew my search was over. How long would I wait until he was ready to sell? As I prepared to exchange my e-mail address with him and complete the transaction for the articles I'd selected, the fellow up and changed his mind!!! I know this may certainly sound strange, but I think that John's spirit may have compelled him to change his mind. So, I asked: "What made you change your mind?" He said my obvious and sincere enthusiasm, for John in particular, made him realize I would be a caring custodian for a piece he had loved too but saw that it was the right time to "let it go". He told me the price as he began to write up a money-back guarantee. Not having quite enough cash on hand, I bolted to the ATM, which the manager of the Beatles Shop gave me directions to: up the stairs and across the street from the shop. "How convenient!" I exclaimed. Leaving my husband behind, probably forgetting he was even there, I extracted pounds (which initially struck me as funny but of course we were in England) enough and raced back to the shop to gladly exchange currency for the "John" signature that is so much more than that to me.

So went the pinnacle of my collecting experiences to date. Naturally, there were other highlights to Liverpool. If you have been there you have seen them too. I just can't say enough about that marvelous day in early June of 1999. It was the finding, the meeting, the people, the place, the provenance and the details of this autograph that make it such a splendid jewel and the most precious in my Beatles collection. My husband noted I was the first to take it out of the country ever. I thought, well, of course! Though keeping it in Liverpool wouldn't necessarily be a burden to me.

In the time since I've owned it, I have insured it along with my other original Beatles memorabilia. I've taken it to different appraisers at different types of shows, Beatles and Non-Beatles and I do have a feel for its market value. I certainly have no reason to be disappointed. The man in Liverpool was no doubt an honest man. I knew he was straight forward just from talking with him. Rest assured, for every one nefarious dealer in Beatles collecting you meet, there are more than plenty like the man I purchased John's autograph from. One appraisal went so far as to refer to it as an artifact! Gear!

Now you ask me if I will ever sell it? As you may have guessed, not likely. For I have added my own story to the life of this piece. I hope you may have realized what is the most precious item in your own collection. But if you haven't found that precious piece, your "Holy Grail", know that, around every corner, at anytime, even when you're not looking, it can be there right in front of you.

Photo believed to be circa 1961
(I have blurred the image to retain its market value as an unpublished photograph)

Signature is from early 1962

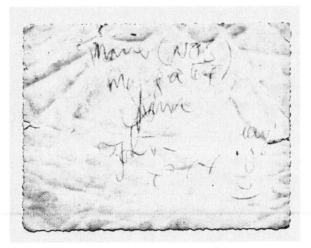

Barely Together, Never Apart

Nearly a year since we were together
We first met
I can't forget
You mean so very much to me.
I felt your history
The places you walked
You were with me
I miss you so dearly
In my darkest times
I want to, need to…run
Back to you
Your loving embrace

Others think you course
Scoff at my attachment
"Get over it, that was the past"
I cannot.
I want your past in my future- always
But I turned around and suddenly
It was a year now
My past is your past
I loved every minute, every second
I couldn't write enough
Then I wanted more
I couldn't stop, soaking, absorbing
All you were
All you are
You will be – in me forever
Locked in the deepest, dearest center of my heart
It beats on and on
To the next time we are together

I made the mistake of letting you in
But it wasn't a mistake
It was destiny
Why did I ever wonder or worry

That your reality would crush my fantasy
Damn you! They made them stronger
And with the fantasies are now memories
Memories of you
You and me
In each other's lives

So many others made the journey
Did they see the things I saw?
They did, but did they feel the things I felt?
What I still incessantly feel for you?
I had to stop, to wipe the tears
So many have I cried for you
So short was our time
So intense
So loving
Even when I was tired and ached
You lingered within
And guided me to comfort, to rest
When I couldn't stop just loving you

As you faded into the horizon
My inevitable departure
I said to you from those sacred places in my heart
"I'll be here to love you again"
You said, "I'm here, I'm waiting"
And I gave you a name
Tripped over in my mind
As pen put to journal paper
Just as you would
And you know your own name
From me to you
With all I am - you are
My Loverpool

The ending
Is but a beginning
To the next time we are one
And while we are apart
We are not
You are here
I am there
Our memory of one another held and cherished
We connect on that plane of Love
And it is that we are never apart
Now we go forward
Together

CHAPTER

TO

II 's

Love is 20/20

Those Eyes
So long have I looked
And still I see more
With mine

Your eyes
Deep, penetrating
No lies can I tell
To them

So intense
Soul full
Of your Spirit
Eternity
I am lost
In them forever

Omni in sight
Full of wisdom
They are
My lover's
Lifetimes ago
Once only
For me

You See!

Physically myopic
Accused dyslexic
But reality
Knows better
I know
I am myopic too

Your tired
Wise eyes see
The truth
Of 20/20 Love
It is all
We are all
Love

Each one
Alone
And Together
We soar
Unstoppable
And powerful
Yet muted

They all know it
Why don't they
See it too?
The distractions
Endless
External attractions
Have blinded
The ability
To see
Themselves within

To find what is there
The truth
You see so clearly
Love inside
Everyone

I Look At You

I look at you
All I see is
Love
Everything else is
Nothing
The years of anger
The hurt
The pain
Nothing else
But
Love
Why?
I wonder
You and not
Another
Only you
Do these things
To me
At times
I am overwhelmed
By your looks
But that's only the invitation
To see what lies beneath
Within
So true
So pure
SO...intense!
And THAT blows my mind
You never gave me anything else
Though I tried to twist it
So many twisted,
Deceptive ways
Yet you remained
Consistent
Unconditional

Love
Thank you
For waiting so long
So very long
For me to accept it
Embrace it
Now it allows me
To embrace you
All of you
Unconditionally
And I return freely
What has been given to me
From you as freely
For these many years
And we are one
Within the Love
Together.

A Querious State

The air is thick with you
How could I know these emotions?
What you said or not
How is that possible?
Are we so connected?
So in tune
Why are you sharing
For me to experience
So much
I cried, though you were
Seemingly happy
It is the past
Yet why does it so profoundly
Affect me?
My sensitivities are peaked
Like a tight wire
You plucked the string and
My mind
Felt the emotion reverberate
The vibration across time and space
The sensations do not frighten
Upon reflection they soothe
The tears merely a response
To the literal flood of emotion
My intuitive sense tingles
Senses heightened
Is this how it feels?

To be aware
So aware
Of another's feelings
Do you occupy a space
So deep in my heart that
What I feel
When I see the old films
Is actually you?
You responding
to what you see through
ME?

CHAPTER

TO

LOVE

Get Real, Love!

Help!
Eight days a week
I write in my own right
To please, please me
Oh yeah
I'll get you!

Let me take you
Down to a place
I'm going to
In my mind
When I am
Alone without you
Thinking
Ask me why

I don't want to
Spoil the party
Imagine!
I'm only sleeping
She said, he said
Love is the word

Free as a bird
In my life
Cause I couldn't stand
Drinking her wine
I should have known better
Yeah, yeah, yeah
You can't do that!

Aisumasen
I just did it
Like starting over
We love you
And it's all you need
From me
To you
But I'll be back again

Love Only, Love

I was only four
When you sang those words
About all you need
I believe them today
As I did then
Now and ever more
No truer words were spoken
Ever!
No words easier to understand
So why
Why?
Are they so hard to follow
Why are the simplest things
Too hard
To do
Because they are-
Simply hard
Hardly simple
So basic though
Just to love
ALL
Is needed
For me
From me
For you
From you
To you
That's all we need
All to do

Soldier for Love

Surrender yourselves
The power of Love
Is unconquerable
It survives
Cannot be extinguished
Many have tried only
To find the fight
Is useless, pointless

Surrender to Love
To peace
The struggle is over
If you choose
Say "yes"

You can
You will
One day
Some day
Do not wait
Til you are old and wise
Be foolish
Be in the now
Be Love
And you
Already have

Drink on, Luv

I am drunk
The sweet nectar
Of your voice
In my ears
The memory of the last time we spoke
Together those words.

Your face
The flash of your eyes
I see them in my memory too
I see them now in a vision
How do you do that

Take me there with you
Where you go
No matter of course to me
Just with you
That's ALL that counts
Are you all I need

Yes is my reply
Because you are not
Speaking of love
You ARE Love

I feel you wrapping around me
The touch without fingers
Embraces me full
My heart sings in your arms
Now, your voice in song

I already hear the song in my thoughts
To hear it as recorded
So long ago
Those words so sung
I love them
Say them again and again

Yes that is good…
If you had fallen
I would've been true
No pain for us
How could I hurt you

Take me as ever my lover
As always and forever
I shall be yours
Yours
YOURS!

CHAPTER

TO

STEP BEYOND

Sounds of a Time

The message of words
Drift in the air
Across time
Across space
The sound
To my ears
Is a dream away
A world I've known
But never lived
The spirit
The mind
All as one
Forever within

The Center

To stand in the center
Of your essence
Why do I forget
Stray from there
The golden warmth
Of your shining soul
Blending with mine
This is peace
The place to be
One and everyone
Remind me always

I let you go
You let me grow
And somehow you are
Still here
This is Love
Beyond convention
Beyond this place
We know as Earth
In eternity lies
The essence of
The Universal us

Tell me again,
Love
Have Fun
Write
Share-on

Now Is The Time

Now is the time
We are here together
All others gone
From the physical plane
I transcend
You descend
And we are one
Again
In thought

Creating with love
The fancies
Of our imaginations
You did not know
Yes you did too
I know you are
I feel it
Through my fingers
In my mind
In my time
Alone
With you

The cherished moment
Grown to the now
More than a flicker
In my plane
The plane you once walked
And knew me not
Then I found you
But you had always been here

I only needed to feel
What I didn't see
What is so plain today
I wonder how I was so blind
For so long
To the love so eternal
Awaiting only
My discovery
Of you with me

Of our creativity
Inspired from the past
Pointing to the future
From the now
John,
Let us continue...

Letting Grow

Just because I know
We are one
Is how I know
I can now let you go

With love I release you
Our eternal souls
Are never truly apart
The time is now
Yet we are only timeless
So it is natural we are ever-present

CHAPTER

OF

ART

In My Own Opinion- an Art Show Review

I certainly had a smile on my face as I reviewed the many artworks of John's for sale at a benefit/exhibit. One of the earliest pieces was a drawing from 1966 similar to the fat budgie from "Spaniard", John had signed this one. Also from the early period (1964) was a print of the now famous "Free as A Bird" drawing and I recalled how Pete Shotton remembered it in his book and said the young fellow was him. The famous Bag One prints were there, along with the erotic ones. The descriptions noted that Yoko did not pose for these drawings. John had drawn them from his own imagination. Not surprising from someone who left us with the number one song of the millennium, "Imagine".

Nearly all of the pieces have been shown before and written about. I have read about them and seen them through books in the past. However, the act of seeing them large, framed and in show format allows you to experience them as opposed to simply viewing them in a book. In this case size and being live does matter. The show covered all periods of John's artwork, mid-sixties forward, including prints from the book <u>John Lennon Real Love- the Drawings for Sean</u>. All in color, they have a child's whimsy to them and invoke the memories and imagination of being five or six all over again for me.

What I found especially tender were the drawings of their family life. On the couch, John, Yoko and Sean. Yoko on the phone as she and John look on with love at Sean playing on the floor. A scene of the three of them at tea in Japan was also sweet. The one that I loved the most though, and probably because I am the mother of my own beautiful boy, was the drawing of Yoko kneeling as Sean, a little over a year old, toddles across the room into the open, waiting arms of his mother. John, like many artists, catches the most sincere snatches of time in these drawings. His style, open and flowing, allows us to fill-in our own details if we like. In my case they were feelings, overwhelmingly, of love.

Some of the prints were whimsical, some had hidden meaning. Fortunately, all the works were noted with a degree of interpretation and those who have studied his art can surely lay more analysis to it. I enjoyed the show for the good feelings it sparked in me and the giggles it brought and naturally, the love. Not to overindulge, but two other drawings stood out for me as well. The print of John and Yoko under the tree, no doubt inspired by the photo and cover of the album "Plastic Ono Band", spoke peace and happiness to me. It reminded my husband of "Grow Old with Me", though not created at the same time he was accurate in the reference.

Finally, the drawing that became the covering for John's Musical Anthology. "He Tried to Face Reality", I found to be moving in that it speaks to the human struggle, daily, to reconcile how we want to see the world and how it really is. As individuals we all see things just a little different and it's drawings like this that lead us to question but also give comfort somehow. Well, that's how I feel anyway. One final series of offerings were the lithographed lyrics to a number of his songs, a set from the Beatles years and a set from his solo years, again all beautifully framed. We are so very fortunate to have so much of John's work, whether written, musical or pictorial, available to love.

CAVERN COLLECTABLES
(with an 'A')
crafted by
Sharon Richards

Inspired by the very famous Liverpool venue, I created this 1/12" scale shop which I imagine to own life-size- perhaps one day. My shop has many one of a kind items. Other items you may recognize or have "full scale" in your own collection. It took me about 2 months to build this room box which measures 18" wide, 15" high and 13" deep. Most of the contents are built from scratch. The exceptions are the chandelier, chairs and the round display table. Where did I get my original idea to do a shop like this? In a dream, from a Mister Beatle man on a flaming pie, of course!

Enjoy browsing the shop. See if you can find things lying about that are referenced in Beatle songs. Though they may be harder to see in the picture than in person. Have fun!

This room box won first place- amateur category in the 1999 Orlando Beatlefest Art Show.

SONGS OF A Beatle JOHN
crafted by
Sharon Richards

This 3-D Shadow box contains many of my favorite John songs. Only ¾" of an inch deep. One of the miniatures inside is worth nearly $100.00 alone (the kaleidoscope). See if you can figure out all the songs being showcased. `It took me only a couple of hours to put this one together. The hardest part was finding all the little items to represent the songs. And yes! That is a real corn flake the walrus is sitting on. But enough of my hints...

CHAPTER

TO

FICTION

DISCLAIMER

The following essay is pure fiction. It in no way attempts to accurately represent any events in a period of John Lennon's life. The author does not seek in this essay to disrespect Mr. Lennon. Nor does she claim to have any knowledge of events or behaviors other than those that can be extracted from any of the numerous public interviews, magazine articles and non-fiction books currently in print or previously published in the past about the Beatles and John Lennon. The author only seeks to entertain by way of fantasy a fictional tale, which was inspired by a popular song written by John Lennon and recorded by the Beatles.

A VERY UNTRUE STORY

Fireplace now ablaze, it began to warm the main room of the chateau. I headed over to a set of the large long windows, opposite either side of the fireplace, to see if he was coming. Before I got half way to the couch, barely crossing the rug in front of the hearth, I heard that deep velvet accent at my door. John knew it made me crazy, hot when he spoke the unacceptable derivative coupled with his chosen pet name for any woman he desired, "Lizzie, luv. I've come to chat ya up like ya wanted." He didn't need to knock. The door was open by the time he'd got the word 'love' out of his mouth. I was delighted that he got away. So many nights after the dailies it was all the four of them could do but giggle their way to bed. They did seem to have a voracious appetite for their latest indulgent, reefer. I figured in a way, they had a right, pressures of fame and all. He cockily staggered in and he had three bottles of Bordeaux in his arms. How many were in him already along with however as many joints, I could only imagine. He had his guitar slung across his back, the black strap crossing his chest. He had no coat or cap and his boots were untied. Warm enough in his black jeans and turtleneck sweater I guess. He always looked so sexy in black, even though he was so...

Seeing the wine, I had a momentary flashback to many a college weekend. But I'd had a vast variety, for better or worse, of booze and drugs since then too. He smiled his stupid -I know what you need- grin and gave me a kiss as he put down the wines on the counter. "Got your note, luv. Didn't make ya wait too bloody long I hope."

I shook my head. "Well, I just felt like some conversation, no interview. I really wasn't inviting any more than that." I opened a bottle, poured myself a glass and delighted in the fermented fruit drink.

"I know Lizzie... just talk. I do need ta. Ya know how I love ya. Besides you're the only reporter I can hang out with who doesn't ask arsenine questions. If ya even have any now. Shit, sometimes you'd think I was the bloody reporter, some of the questions I ask ya." We chuckled at the last part of his comment as he slipped off the six-string and leaned it against the couch.

"Yeah, I suppose. If any one of my reporter friends knew how we are alone in conversation, I 'd probably become more a part of the story than being able to report it.", I reasoned. "And really John, I'm quite bored with writing the image all our papers spout, anyway. The smart one, the cute one, quiet and sad ones, as if you guys weren't stand alone people. Just parts of a whole, one trait for you and one each for the others. Brian started it, you bought into it and he encourages it and so the shit happens, so what! Do you have any idea how much the fans buy it?" He busted out laughing at my statement of fact agreeing with what I said.

Admitting by my own snicker what I'd just said I continued, "You must admit that you, Paul, George and Ring have had so much thrown at you so fast. It's got to be gear to have somebody to talk to that isn't caught in the madness, isn't it? That's part of why you keep coming back to be with me. Because I remember the not-so-fab five of the Grosse Ferenheit, right? Fame is fucked up and moving too fast, you've said that to me more than once. The media and public may see you as a god or dream weaver, but me? Shit John! You're only human!" I don't know why I suddenly felt compelled to remind him that he doesn't need to buy into all the hype he was buried in. Maybe it was because I wanted to save him. Desperately! I could see what was happening and knew he was heading for a nervous breakdown -one day. Not today but someday...that would be a day. Would I want to be there, for him? Yes, if I was allowed to do something. Definitely! But if it happened at a press conference, a public place, and I merely had to watch. Restrained from doing anything then sadly- no. That's why I just wanted to talk to him tonight. In our last real conversation he was so pressed to control anything about his life and I empathized.

I went to the counter to refill my wineglass and turned to head over to the couch. Crossing to me and looking lovingly into my eyes he said quietly, "Ya seem to be one of the few people in my life to recognize I'm just a person. Why is that?"

I looked thoughtfully into his sadly glazed over cinnamon brown eyes and took his hand to hold mine. "Well John, I'm not exactly your auntie but it could be that I knew you before you was the way you was then before now the way you is now?"

He dropped my hand and wrapped me in a bear hug as he laughed at my turn of phrase from the recent weeks of filming. Warmed, and mutually comforted by the embrace, I added, "But then you know things are a lot different now than they were in Hamburg." He broke away and shot out irritated, revealing the base of his altered state of mind and the source of his immediate anger.

"Well, what the hell difference does it make anyway! I know what's goin' on too! Why does everybody gotta be hangin' about while we're making this part of the movie? I see what's happenin'! I...know who it's with! Fuck! Or maybe I don't know... but it isn't right. I've known ya since before ... So that kinda makes ya different, ya know."

I wasn't quite sure what or who he was referring to. He sounded so mixed up and confused and I recognized that. So I took his paranoia with a grain of salt. What he said made some sense I suppose. No more than what he felt I was saying, I guess. Regardless, I was so glad he took my invite. I think we both needed the conversational release.

"Know what Lizzie? I think I know what ya're getting at about life happening. No matter what I do it seems ta happen even if I don't want it to. See?"

"I know I believe it. No more did it become apparent to me than the first time I happened on the Reeperbahn."

"Shit, yeah", he said in realization.

I hated to bring it up but I did anyway, in a joking way, but it wasn't how he took it. "Hell, someday I may finally find that Mr. Right, John."

Suddenly he was all serious in his face, the drugs and liquor accentuating his reaction to my words, "I'll be the soddin' sap then. I suppose once you find your fuckin' Mr. Right that will be it, eh?"

I wasn't taken aback by his attitude but I had to admit his place in my life, which he apparently chose to forget for the moment. So I reminded him, "I may find him. But I already found my soul mate! He's married and has a son." His penetrating look returned and drilled deep to my center.

"DAMN IT! I know ya've touched his inner soul Lizzie and he...aarrhh... Fuck it!"

I strove to lighten the mood, which was heading into a depressing descent of self-pity on both our parts so I concluded.

"Well, we need to be happy with what has been and what will come. Whatever the outcome! It's not right now-but later who the hell can know? Only God or whatever is having a jolly time watching over us."

He spurted out his raw emotions, "Shit! I want ya Lizzie, but I'm so confused."

I ran my fingers through my long hair, flipping it back and plopped on to a barstool near the counter. Both of us were exhausted from the day and by the conversation. Seeing an idea in his eyes I watched as he, still standing, dug into his pants pocket, produced a joint and lighting it offered me a drag. Then for whatever got into him, he suddenly hopped on my lap attempting to give me another hug. Not realizing the force of his actions and my lack of resistance to it, I felt us loosing our balance. I clenched the joint in my teeth as we both toppled off the small stool and fell to the floor by the couch and on to the rug. Still holding each other, we rolled around and busted out laughing. I passed back the reefer to John. Then looking over to see the bar stool in a less than useful state, I giggled "Well I guess the company's gonna dock me for that but I don't think I'll tell them HOW it happened."

Releasing the smoke of his drag he recalled, "Nah luv, ya once kept me from bein' docked, least I can do is return the favor."

I thought, that'll be fab he'll get someone in the entourage to buy another, but my thoughts stopped cold as I watched what he did next. Continuing his own fits of laughter he broke the stool into smaller pieces and tossed them in the fireplace. Oh shit! John did have a knack for the unexpected. He flopped on the rug in a heap looking at the fire- I followed. He took another drag off the reefer and passed it to me. In his way he was heading, more directly than me, to the goal we suddenly both had in mind, to loose our minds in the bevy of mood altering resources available to us. The discussion got a little heavy and I was ready to relieve a bit of tension too. I took a good long toke on the joint. Rolling the smoke in my mouth, I slowly inhaled it into my lungs, exhaled and let the tiniest amount of smoke go in a light puff. This was high quality weed! As John and I enjoyed the flames of the broken, burning stool he blurted, "Burns good, eh luv?" Snickering at his own juvenile delinquency, I couldn't help but echo his laughter. Continuing the silliness, we reveled in our destruction of rented furniture, at my company's expense. Funnier still was the thought that it would be cleared away next time the chimney sweep carried out his duties. Within minutes, the main area of the chateau we occupied not only contained the fireplace's scent of burning wood, but also was thick with the joint's scent of sweet smoke. I heaved a big sigh of relief and for whatever reason, it made John snicker. Then the snickering turned to giggling and blossomed into all out gut busting laughter from both of us. At what who knows? Only that big being in the sky, we mock-philosophically mused. Putting on his most seriously silly face, he rolled over to where his guitar lay. Then rolling back to me I squealed like one of the teeny-boppers, giggling under my breath, "ooooooo, eeeeeeeee! a Beatle's gonna sing a song just for me, I could just die!!! Oh, John, John please, please yeah, yeah, yeah! OW!" I shot him the opportunity to lash out like he always fancied to do at the screaming girls.

Laughing as he mocked anger, which I knew he could easily turn into true rage, he barked, "If ya'd fuckin' shut the fuck up and stop yare stupid arsinine screamin' ya fuckn' twat I will. Then blow me, an' I'll fuck ya over and then get the fuck out of my life!" Under any other circumstance, I could take that horrid display quite personally and it wasn't especially funny, except that all the intoxicants we'd consumed made it almost hysterical. So I shut the hell up and he proceeded to play the guitar atop his head and sang to the tune of 'She Loves You', "We're fucked up yeah! yeah! yeah!, Ya think ya lost yer mind, well I saw it yesterday. Just laying like a lump ya fuckin' got nuthin' ta say..."

He was playing quite insane and I could barely catch my breath for his re-lyricsing. Then he had to use that incredibly foolish grin of his. I had my own chance though as I had him in fits of gasping laughter by climbing the floor and falling, rolling down back to his lap, screaming and laughing all the way. Again not really that funny, I guess, when you're not high or drunk or ...both. Perhaps because we had been laughing so hard. Or John's strange faces and mine back to him, made me begin to feel a bit warm. Maybe even the fire of fragmented furniture was reason, in part. Almost too warm really. Rather likely though, from the influence of so much pot and wine was why I suddenly felt as if I was on fire.

"Shit John! I need to cool off!" So I began stripping right there and ran to the bathroom to fill the tub with cool water and soap bubbles. Tripping along the way incredibly drunk and flying higher than I ever had. John was still rolling on the floor as I left the room. I heard him laugh saying,

58

"Ya look so bloody stupid, silly there gettin' hot and runnin' Lizzie. Hey Lizzie! Hahaahhahahaah!"

Tossing my clothes to wherever they landed as I went. I guess I was wiggling wildly too and that made him laugh even more. When I finally did get to the bathroom and in the tub of cool soapy water, I let out such a big sigh of relief that it must've interrupted John's giggling from the main room where our nonsense had started. What were we talking about? My thought disintegrated as John appeared fully clothed, at the bathroom door. That ridiculous grin of his and glazed eyes- I knew he was up to no good in his thoughts. How I loved that about him! Busting into another laughing fit of my own I stopped suddenly to scream out, "EEEEKKKK! There's a fully clothed man in my bathroom!! Help! I need somebody Help! John I need ya Johnny..."

Then we both started laughing. John fell to his knees and dunked his head into the tub, rebounding off my middle. That normally would've hurt but I wasn't feeling any pain. The recoil off my body was enough to bring him out again, only his hair and face wet. He laughed and sputtered out the excess water. Leaning into me over the side of the tub he grabbed me and I leaned his way. Kissing amorously only the giggles eventually parting our lips. "Ya're so fucked up Lizzie luv! Just look at ya! Won't ya ever grow up??"

"When you do my albern junge!" I gasped between laughs. Everything seemed so much more intense.

"Fuckin' silly am I? I'm not the one who tore off me clothes uncontrollably, trippin' and wiggling like some bloody flopping fish out of water gettin' in here!"

Then before I knew it he poured himself into the bath, clothes and all, with me and began to tickle me everywhere and all at once so that I could barely get out my thoughts. "John! Bloody hell! I have to work in the morning!" And then I couldn't stop laughing for his tickling torture the pot and booze making me fly.

"Ya drive me bloody mad when yer squirmin', luv. It gets me so fucked and excited." Well, then I just had to yell for more, more, MORE! Then I began a backlash attack on him though I had the greater challenge. I had to remove the wet clothing. I wasn't too successful but I got at what I wanted and started tickling him. He kindly removed his bulky sweater, ten times heavier now that it was wet, as I peeled the last garment from his body. Then 'SMAK!' as he twisted the black sweater into a whip to intentionally slap me on the ass, which ended up closer to hitting me in the head because I tried to get out of the way, but not quick enough. Looking each other over and the great volume of water we had expelled from the tub we couldn't help, of course, laughing. He started the water running again. This time the water was a bit warmer and we felt the effects of the reefer we had shared calm just a bit. Still snickering though we got back into the tub and started at one another again.

"I'm so hungry, luv." he abruptly commented.

"I've got the crave on for a snack myself." I giggled.

Like a shot he was out of the bathroom and sprinted to the kitchen. Reappearing in what seemed an instant with an assortment of items; crackers, cheese, chips, chocolate, seemed anything he could get his hands on and more... wine! "This should cover tit, I mean it." He laughed.

"John, get in here! I meant I want you!" I was in a dreamy daze. He complied as willingly as when I stated what he thought was a desire for edibles. Laughing loudly at my comment he said, "Leave some of me at least, luv, if you don't mind." He grabbed a handful of the goodies he had carried in and sat in the tub, slouching.

"Don't worry", I said laughing, "I only want to taste for a long while." Nearly dropping his wine he shuddered with his chill of delight.

"Oh god, Lizzie! I'm glad ya're into English food."

"Any time, my love." I held my head up briefly. "Wine please?"

He proceeded to grant my request by spilling a quantity of the contents into my open mouth. Though he poured so close to his chest, that I did have to lick and slurp some of it off him and I knew he meant to do that. Refreshed, I returned now to what I craved. He was arching, moaning, nearly climbing the walls of the tub and then laughing too. "Damn, that feels so fuckin'...ack What the fuck ya got in there. French ticklers? AHA!! Oh! Ahh! Lizzie! I don't fuckin' care. Take it all, luv! Whatever ya want!"

Again, water was slopping on to the bathroom floor. Who cared! Certainly not us.

"John, everything's so much more intense, I feel more present than ever. And you're talking so much. I love it. I love your voice. The sound of it's so hot, so intense the more you say the more I want to continue."

"Well, don't stop now, luv, and I won't either!"

Nearly the entire volume of water was again slopped out on the floor. Sitting up to catch my breath, I thought I'd take my turn to refill the tub. Then suddenly I was pounced upon by the raging animal of John. Giggling and growling all at once, "My turn now ya naughty girl!" Bringing the intended target closer to his face, John held me close by the waist and proceeded.

"What have YOU got in there love?" I asked giggling and deathly curious. He did not speak now, but his actions removed the mystery as he reached for another chocolate. He drew me nearer to melt the sweet in his mouth into my flaming passion.

When at last he paused, sitting back to catch his own breath. I scrambled out of the bath and attempted to give chase for added excitement. But he was much the aggressor this night, having started his high long before me. He took me down just as I made it back to the rug in front of the fireplace where our strange conversation had ended much earlier. We had both forgotten towels to dry off. Oh well! Looking at me with those wildly drunk and high eyes of his, they tried to prepare me for the force of what was to come. The strength of his advance took my breath away and I could not offer any resistance. I cried out and he grunted back.

We rode the combined highs of lovemaking, pot, food and wine all at the same time. The colors were incredible. Swirling reds, floating blues, gleaming whites, green streaks and orange marmalade swaths, floating, co-joining and melding around us into the feelings of hot passion, love and ecstasy. Were we still corporeal? We always did manage to surprise each other with the intensity of passion we could both produce from one another- for one another. His capacity to reach to my inner core and my gaining ability to thrust back equal power to his thrust consistently produced more explosive results each time we shared our love. I felt our bodies melding together in the most intimate of ways. It seemed our spirits mingled, mixing outside our bodies. Our bodies moving as the ultimate united sexual beings. So this is another way to dry off after a bath!

Now, after the fiery explosion of passion there was not a second. How could it be possible for either of us? We had so much emotion, so intense and both of us were fully exhausted. All the agents of mood altering used up in our mutual expressions of deep soulful love, understanding and tender, yet passionate and erotic on the edge simultaneously. Then lying there on his chest, in the glow of the fireplace, I cuddled close to kiss him. Kissing back he nipped my ear, "Never fails when ya let yer knickers down, luv…"

"Yeah, you too…" I fell asleep listening to his heartbeat. The last cracklings of the fire calming with our passions. I always slept so peacefully with John. Most likely the result of depleted energy but a satisfying feeling as well. I knew he felt the same.

I woke up at my normal work time despite the evening that had just ended. I can live on two hours sleep, no problem! More amazing still was the way I felt. Expecting "hair of the dog" to plague my day, I looked to the brightness entering the long windows with not so much as a flinch. I felt in tune with the world, not a hangover in site. Not even so much as a headache. What a glorious day! I said to myself. I did not want to wake John as he was still quite out from his visit to chat me up. I giggled at that thought as he repositioned. Perhaps he was waking up? But then only a heavy sigh and...snoring!!?? Good heavens John! Well, now I really could not stop the urge to burst out laughing but somehow I did. Quietly, I dressed to make my way to another day of entertainment reporting. Unlikely my chat with John would make it anywhere near page one or page twenty-one for that matter. I walked out with John sleeping au natural on the rug. I did take care to cover him with the blanket off the still made, untouched bed of my guest chateau. Then I tried to wake him. All I got for response was, "Nah goin' fuckin' class, sot."

OOOKAY!

"I love you too!" I whispered kissing him.

Leaving him a note I said:

'John love-

Told you I had to work in the morning. See you on the set!

Love, Lizzie (your dizzy miss)'

A Lover's Apology

Dreaming of words
My thoughts to purge
On paper I must
Express my lust
In great detail about one extraordinary man

Thoughts crass they may be
I can't help it you see
Because honest and true
Is the passion I offer to you
In this text of unseemly events

My emotions run deep
And these thoughts as I sleep
Keep me writing in here
Of a love so sacred and dear
So it isn't as perverse as you'd think

For when telling the truth
Even when uncouth
No diplomacy satisfies
And the expressions will seem lies
While engaged in the realm of the heart

When pure love is the cause
You must listen and pause
For you realize deep inside
You cannot deride
Because you once felt this way too
About someone you knew

So please don't malign
Please just resign
And let my tale be told
Without barriers- brash and bold
For love's expression cannot be compromised

Youngblood

John
You are so wild
And strong
I love your vitality
I am enchanted again
By the younger
The elder is sage
The intellect of once
In a millennium
But it is your young,
Raw, passionate
Rockcr sclf
Began the tale
These past days
Seeing it displayed
Though sometimes inaccurately
Compressed for time's sake...

STILL!!!
The juices got flowing
All that I do know
You know what I mean...
The way you looked
Yeah, you know
It's all you got to do
In leathers
The younger
Standing there
The first sight

Cinnamon brown and glazed
Eyes
Aquiline and fresh
Features
Slicked and messed
Hair

The reality of you
Induces the fantasy
Imagination rooted there
Then the rest
All it is
A relationship
Like no other
I love you for it
And so much more
The heat rises
The body warms
The thoughts of
"Do you have any hobbies?"
OH, What you wrote!
But you
YOU know
What I mean
And all is spoken
Without a syllable
That LOOK
"Come hither, luv"
Your soulful eyes
The day of penetrating gaze
Yeah – I know

CHAPTER

TO

THE END?

How Did He Do THAT!

How can I deny paying lip service to a person that pointed me in the direction of my life's path? Some how, some way there must come out of me a story, an essay some sort of prose to pay homage to the man who started all this upheaval in my life. Or at least to take the bits I have and somehow correlate them into a cohesive text to be understood by all and yet not to sound as thought I've fallen off the sanity wagon. But I think we all must be a little insane to be passionate, truly passionate about something. Write about the way his music makes me feel, specific songs, sure but it's beyond that. Something not to be perceived as praising crap to the point of saccharine. He's still wreaking his influence all over me. Will John always inspire me? Truthfully, I don't think the inspiration will ever stop, this is the influence of a lifetime from the point it started forward, one of those point of no return things. How does one influence a life, inspire creativity to the level of intense passion? Well, however it is done he did it to me. I can honestly say I love him deeply, dearly, for all that he stood for, the way he lived, his own body of works, musical, written and visual. How do you love someone that intensely that you never met? Perhaps I will understand all the psychological reasons of how it happened one day.

Now as for the why...Why? Simply because I needed to have passion, extreme passion, infused into my life. So, it came through music. To discover my life's path, to be there within my heart, in my mind the knowledge I accumulated through reading, to sustain me when all else failed. John dragged me up from the lowest emotional point in my life. Since knowing him, I have not considered suicide seriously. I used to, sadly, on a fairly regular basis. It was awful and for incredibly vain reasons. Therapists, psychoanalysts, psychiatrists they did not cure me. They said my love of the Beatles, and John especially, was a powerful defense mechanism a means to deny my reality. And by acting on and encouraging my love that I was

68

cheating myself out of a fully productive life. I had been diagnosed as a budding alcoholic and eventually, bipolar II. I took drugs like seroquel and depakote. I felt they muted my ability to creatively and passionately express myself.

BUT and that's a big "but", would anyone be remotely interested in how he changed me or rather inspired me to change myself? How close will I come to opening those most sacred places of my heart, where I revel in my feelings for him? We seem to be like-minded creative souls. That John is frequently in my thoughts, that his life has guided me to fulfillment of purpose in mine, can I be so arrogant? Did there have to be so many coincidental things, the more I discovered about him to bring me to this conclusion? Is it important that I prove my beliefs or only important that I believe it? I think the latter is how I truly feel. I am not a pessimist. I would rather think it is his legacy than any other that influences me. I am certain of all the commentary I have done in here. Is this the book to share- about John and his influence and guidance with me? Hopefully, it will sit well with all fans that call him their favorite. I'm hoping you can relate to me. Though I'm not sure how many others will admit the kind of things I have here. John has taught me, in his mediums of word and song, how to love myself and everyone in my life I meet. He helped me become...me. But I don't want to be saccharine to the positive. I have no intention to deify him. That can be offensive. I know it is something he didn't like in life. He wanted us to realize he was just a man, a human being trying his best to be...John. Not a dream-weaver, not the walrus, just John. I only seek to share, to give my due to this amazing person John Lennon.

John, I offer you my heartfelt thanks and gratitude for leading me into the light and wisdom of my inner self. For encouraging me to look there for the answers. To achieve that fulfilling life the doctors said I couldn't have, how to do it and the direction to take.

Going in circles with your eyes closed makes you dizzy. John's music, studying his struggle for self,

69

connecting with his creativity gave me the courage to open my eyes, look inside myself to see all the bad and the good that is me. From that I am building, devoted to a life of stepping each day closer to realizing my destiny. Big stuff? Yes! We ALL have one. And I don't forget along the way all the things I have accomplished already. The thread, I call it the "golden thread" of me. In hindsight it is so easy to see the single consistent thing in my life once I accepted the good and bad in myself and forgave myself of mistakes I had made. I remember times when the golden thread was used for good and when I abused it for ego and vanity. How can I not thank John for giving me the courage to examine these things in me? How can I not be inspired to creatively express the passion I feel for him, through prose, poetry and possibly the epic proportions of novel size?

I hope I've put together something really tasteful, intellectual, creative, loving and just nearly brushing the fringes of controversy here to give him the honor he deserves on a personal level. He said he would write songs about his life, how could he know about yours and mine? He did though because what he spoke of, sang of, drew was so universal. We all experience it a bit differently but the concepts are timeless. I recognize he was not the first person to ever to think or even express himself in those ways. That would be raising him to sainthood. There are plenty of good people in many mediums who have proposed for centuries what he was proposing in his own life. Yet he had his unique way of telling the tale of his experiences, as early as "There is a Place". I write this as with everything regarding John- for the pure love of it. Well, I guess I just answered the question I asked at the beginning of this essay. This collection of my work seems the best way to express my sincerest thanks to John. I hope you have enjoyed some, if not all of this book. Please don't hesitate to contact me via email at: yourhobby.com/dropforgedlennon .

Thank YOU for reading! Imagine to dream away and love, Love LOVE...8^)